TESTI

"Fred has brilliantly and creatively u̲ ̲... ̲ personal transformation; the written word. Fred's insights and thought provoking exercises will change your life. This book is like having Fred on speed dial."

Derrick Shirley - Psychotherapist, Author, Counsellor

"Fred has spoken to our employees many times in the past. He has always left everyone with the tools and desire to be more effective in both their personal and professional lives. He makes an impression and his sessions are talked about years after.

This book should be given to every employee and to all whom you hold dear, as the exercises contained in it will impact every relationship in their life."

J.Raymond O'Kane - National Director, Bank of Montreal

"Fred's previous books have had great impact on my life and relationships and I've read them all several times. The inspiration and exercises in this book have helped me be more effective in my role and, more importantly, in all my relationships, personally and professionally.

Fred's books are always thought provoking, and inspire me to look internally as well as externally for improvement in all aspects of my life"

Raymond Outar – SAS, Business Intelligence Consultant

"I have hired Fred as a speaker and employee trainer numerous times and he has always left my people with an immediate thought provoking impact.

This book is a valuable tool that you can give to your employees as the exercises within it will change how they think about their life and their business"

Mark Kerzner, President,TMG The Mortgage Group Canada Inc.

As senior vice president of British Columbia's 2nd and 3rd most popular ski resorts I have attended and given many presentations over my 25 year career. Fred was inspirational - it was by far one of the best 3 hours I've spent listening to someone else.

He delivers in an educational, impactful and entertaining format. This really is something you can share with your team mates, your friends and family. It just keeps you on the right track.

Michael J. Ballingall - Senior Vice President,
Big White & Silver Star Resort

To order bulk books on a discount for your company,
please contact fred@fredsarkari.com

Published By: www.ZanaBooks.com

This book, or part thereof, may not be reproduced in any form
without written permission by Fred Sarkari.

Library and Archives Canada Cataloging in Publication

Sarkari, Fred © 2012
All rights reserved worldwide
    Quotes To Ignite Your Mind: 101 Exercises that will change
    your Life / Business

ISBN 978-0-9738108-7-5

1. Inspiration. I Title.

Printed In Canada

QUOTES
TO IGNITE
YOUR MIND

'101' Exercises
That Will Change
Your Life / Business

I dedicate this book to you - all the amazing people who make my life truly wonderful.

Every time I turn around I see someone who makes me happy, makes me think and makes me appreciate how truly blessed I am.

I have learned more lessons from you than you will ever know, and in my heart of hearts, I appreciate every single one of you.

With Love,

Fred Sarkari
Inspire – Educate - Execute

~ ~ ~ ~ ~

I've always believed that every journey is more meaningful if it is shared - that is what makes my journey so precious.

I am constantly amazed and grateful for the incredible people I connect with and how our thoughts and energies work together to Inspire, Educate and Execute. Some of these people I interact with on a personal level, others have been a strong presence on my blogs but are people I've never met.

That is why, when I put this compilation of quotes together, I knew people from my life would be part of it, helping me touch the lives of others.

I invite you to come along – let's enjoy this small part of our journey together...

> "To all those who have crossed my path in life,
> I love you for the essence of who you are."
>
> Fred Sarkari

Love is the ability to open your heart to those around you, everyone from a stranger passing by to a lifetime relationship.

Have the courage to let the people you allow into your heart and soul bring out the best in you.

The best in us is there for the purpose of giving. Everything in life has a greater meaning when you are willing to give it away authentically and expect nothing in return. In turn, the world will offer much more than you ever dreamed possible.

In order to receive anything in life, you have to be willing to give it away.

The most intense love you will feel is when you give love.

When you write down the main things you are not willing to lose in life you will see that most of the things you have are for the giving.

"This world needs more compassion."
Fred Sarkari

It is not our job to solve the problems of the world but we do have to strive to make it a better place. Be gentle with the people in your life. Approach everyone with compassion and you will find that even your enemies have some sort of beauty to offer.

Do your best to improve other people's lives. especially the weakest. poorest and the lost among us. You will find out that the love you give is much less than the love you receive.

To truly smell a rose is to embrace its beauty with all your senses present.

Have all your senses present as you <u>slowly kiss your spouse</u> - as you <u>listen intently to your children</u> as they chatter through multiple topics all at once. Have all your senses present as you take a full slow breath and <u>feel the love all around you.</u> Don't be like everyone else who says I will start tomorrow. Start living your plan right now.

"A world without color
is like food without taste."

Natasha Chinoy
(My 13 year old niece)

I too often see adults living and doing things just for the sake of doing them and getting them done.

I hope I never lose the child in me when I 'grow up.'

Write down

3 things that you consistently do in your life.

How can you add more color and taste to it?

"I would rather live poor and spend time with my family then be rich and not see them at all."

Zal Chinoy
My 11 year old nephew

I love spending time with my parents. my sister who loves me so much. grandparents who spend time with me. and Freddie mamma, my uncle who plays with me.

I hope everyone out there has so much love. I know I do and I am very fortunate.

Write down

What are you fortunate and grateful for?

Notes

"The unexamined life is not worth living."

Socrates

EXERCISE

Put one hour aside and <u>write down</u> on 2 separate pieces of paper:

- All the good things in your life.
- All the things you want to change in your life.

Spend more time on the good things and simply start changing the things you want to change.

Only by having the courage to look inward, without tainted eyes, can you live a life of honesty and be true to yourself and those around you.

"If you would win a man to your cause, first convince him that you are his sincere friend."

Abraham Lincoln

1. Make a list of your clients & employees.
2. Ask yourself with complete honesty:

   a. Do they believe you are looking out for their best interests?
   b. Do they believe you are a sincere friend to them?

The human mind's greatest need is to be understood.

Care enough to open your heart, understand people for who they are and who they want to be, and, in turn, you will surround yourself with people who will go above and beyond for your cause.

Notes

"A mind troubled by doubt cannot focus on the course to victory."

Arthur Golden,
Memoirs of a Geisha

Only you know, deep within, what you are capable of doing and becoming. Stop letting others pour doubt into your veins.

Create 2 columns:

① People who fuel your potential.
② People who feed your doubt.

"Let no one ever come to you without leaving better and happier."

Mother Teresa

EXERCISE

This one question will change every relationship in your life. Ask yourself right after every interaction,

"How did I make them feel?"

Do this with the next 5 people you talk to. That, my friends, is the beginning of true success.

Notes

> "That's what I consider true generosity.
> You give your all, and yet you always feel
> as if it costs you nothing."
>
> Simone de Beauvoir

The more we collect in our lives the less we cherish what we have.

In chasing more there comes a time when we lose sight of the priorities in our lives.

Walk through your house and pile up everything that you no longer use or need. Collect the extra toys and together as a family share them with those who would cherish them.

Make a list

Of all the precious people in your life – personal and professional
Beside each of them, write down what you can give them that is not materialistic and how you can put a smile on their face based on who they are, the situation they are in, their dreams, their aspirations...
If you cannot answer these questions you know you have become disengaged with those who matter in your life.

> "Always adhere to the values that were instilled in your upbringing"
>
> Carmen Sparg

EXERCISE

Our upbringing is unique to us all – some full of beauty and guidance and others a path of uncertainty – but we always know deep inside the difference between what is right and wrong.

<u>**Write down**</u>:

- 5 qualities/virtues you value the most in life.

- Now circle the one that resonates most within you.

- Ask yourself, are you living this everyday?

- How can you live it more authentically?

"We do not remember days,
we remember moments."

Cesare Pavese

EXERCISE

Nothing else in life exists during the moment my niece and nephew tell me "I love you".

What really matters is often sitting across from us at the breakfast table.

Make 2 lists:

1. The moments you live for.
2. The moments that are passing you by.

"Some say if you do not succeed, try something else, I say if you do not succeed, DO IT AGAIN."

Fred Sarkari

EXERCISE

Where would you be now if you gave up trying to walk the first time you fell on your diapers?

It is not what we have given up in life - it is what more are we going to give up on in life.

Next time you feel like giving up, remind yourself that success is always on the other side of failure.

Make A List

Make a list of things and people you are not willing to give up on.

Notes

"Drive thy business or it will drive thee."

Benjamin Franklin

We become entrepreneurs so that we can live our lives as we wish but we long for success so badly that we often become a slave to our own business, which, in turn, results in losing our freedom.

<u>Write down:</u>

3 things that monetize your business.

- Spend 80% of your time on these.

- Delegate the rest.

"Don't part with your illusions.
When they are gone, you may still exist,
but you have ceased to live."

Mark Twain

The greatest things in history have come about through creativity.

This creativity grows from imagination. The foundation of imagination is built on the illusions we have in our hearts as children.

As adults, when we let go of our illusions, we let go of the creative child within us.

Want to have some fun in life?
Then share your illusions with those around you.

- We all have our fun illusions
- <u>Write out</u> as many as your heart can visualize
- keep writing them, as you never know what will come out of them.

Notes

"Today is yesterday's tomorrow,
and today is tomorrow's yesterday.
Today is your best opportunity to redeem
your past and to make a great future!"

Randy Carney
Minister

What is happening in your life today is in part because of the decisions you made yesterday. What will happen in your life tomorrow will be shaped, in part, by what you do today.

1. Write one critical decision you are going to make today that will impact your tomorrow.

2. Remember, the smaller the acts the more impact they have in our lives tomorrow.

"Designing your product for monetization first and people second will probably leave you with neither."

Tara Hunt

No business will thrive without taking care of its people first.

1.) Make a list of your people.

2.) What is the most important thing to them in your relationship together?

3.) What specifically are you doing to cultivate that?

EXERCISE

Notes

"Creativity can solve almost any problem.
The creative act, the defeat of habit by originality,
overcomes everything."

George Lois

1. Write down the strategies you are implementing right now.

2. Ask yourself, 'how can I make each of them more creative, more original?'

People want a break from the ordinary, so give it to them.

"I don't know the key to success, but the key to failure is trying to please everybody."

Bill Cosby

Every act and every thought you have involves energy. By trying to please everyone you deplete all your energy.

On The Notes Page

1. Quickly, without any deliberation, list where all your energy is expended on a daily basis.

2. Put an 'x' beside each spot that you know is a waste of your energy.

"When was the last time you did something for the first time?"

David Gabb

Life rushes by with everyday tasks but, when you think about it, when was the last time you put yourself out of your comfort zone and did something for the **first** time?

Children do it every day so why, as adults, have we stopped exploring new things?

Write down:

1. The last time you did something for the **first** time.

2. What will you do next for the **first** time?

"It's not enough just to write down your goals, also make a list of how they will change your life."

Melonie Dodaro

Write down the following:

1. A list of your goals.
2. All of the ways your life will improve when you achieve them.
3. All of the ways your life will be impacted in a negative way if you do not achieve them.

This will allow you to decide whether they are important enough to take the action necessary to achieve your Critical goals.

"Life isn't about destiny or purpose. Life is about creating meaning with those around us."

Mike Hassard

EXERCISE

There was a time when I believed in destiny and purpose. What I found out was that although my destiny might give me the drive to get things done it didn't seem to give me fulfillment.

As I get older I have come to realize that the power of touching others is the real "meaning" of life.

1. Write down the most important people in your life.
2. How have you touched their lives lately?

> "The bigger you dream, the smaller
> your obstacles look."
>
> Fred Sarkari

As children we believe we can do and be anything. Then, there comes the first time we are told we cannot - and we come to believe it. Choose this moment, right now, to start to believe that you once again can.

Just believe and your life will change forever.

Write down:

One part of your life where you want to stretch at being better.

"The vitality of thought is in adventure. Ideas won't keep. Something must be done about them."

Alfred North Whitehead

I have met so many wise people who have amazing ideas. It is a sad thought that most of them will be buried with all those ideas still locked within them.

① Write down any and all ideas you have ever had.

② Beside each, list what would be required in order to move them forward.

③ Decide which one you want to start with and, for crying out loud, just start!

"It is by acts and not by ideas that people live."

Anatole France

E
X
E
R
C
I
S
E

A person's true character is revealed when the values they talk about are tested. Unfortunately most people do not even know what they truly value. How can you live something you are not even aware of?

Ask yourself:

1. What are all the things I value in myself?

2. What have I done today to prove it so?

Notes

"The first step to getting the things you want out of life is this: Decide what you want."

Ben Stein

I wish someone had taken the time to just sit with me when I was a child and help me find the courage to write down what I really wanted in life.

It is never too late to start.

<u>Write down</u> whatever comes to mind about what you want in your life - material and non-material.

"No one is ever truly healed – we are all wounded or broken in some way. Its about having relationships with people who accept you as you are, battle scars and all. With that love and support we gain the desire, courage and strength to deal with each issue one at a time and become better people"

Deanne Collinson

Quit waiting around to either become or find Mr/Ms perfect! Its the acceptance, cherishing and loving of the imperfections in others and ourselves that truly help us become the people we desire to be and have in our lives.

1. Write down what you believe are your imperfections.

2. Now start loving them with all your heart.

In doing so, you will find that others will love them as well.

"Do not wait for that perfect opportunity - start running and either the opportunity will catch you or you will catch up to it."

Fred Sarkari

The most important thing to do is <u>create momentum</u> which in turn <u>creates the energy</u> that <u>pushes you forward.</u>

Just like a surfer catching a wave, you have to start paddling with all your might or that perfect wave will go right by you.

(Write down:)

- Every instance that comes to mind where you know you wanted to start moving forward but, for what ever reason (excuse), have not.

- Circle 2 of them

- Spend at least 15 minutes on either one of them each day.

"Sometimes we shine so bright that others have a hard time seeing us".

Natalya Patrick
(At 5 years old)

We have all had those moments in our lives where we could feel ourselves glowing. Our brilliance, love and uniqueness come from within.

Write down:

- Those glowing moments you have experienced.

- If you can't think of any think again because there most certainly was a time.

- What was it that made you shine then?

Notes

"Try not to become a man of success but rather to become a man of value."

Albert Einstein

All the money and fortune in the world cannot replace the wealth behind the value of your name.

Write Down

(What do you want to be known for?)

Answer that first and everything else will fall into place.

"Real success is finding your lifework in
the work that you love."

David McCullough

Write down

Everything you love about the work
that you do right now.

No matter what the work is, if you
cannot find a list of things you love
about it, know that is a sign that
your present state of mind will not
find love in anything.

Notes

"If we cannot laugh enough at the little
moments with the ones we love,
what do we live for anyway?"

Fred Sarkari

How, at times, I miss those pure moments of laughter with the ones I love.

The courage to live for those moments is what it means to live a fulfilling and beautiful life.

Write down:

1. all the times that come to mind where you had the best laughter filled moments with your loved ones.

- Go relive those moments with them in the form of a dialouge

2. What is your most precious thing to do with your loved ones.

- Just make more time for it. Do not let those moments be put on a shelf

"Pleasure in the job puts perfection in the work."

Aristotle

1. Write down all the things that annoy you at your job / business.

2. Write down the good and pleasurable things beside them.

Loving what you do is a state of mind. Change how you look at your work and pleasure will flow within it.

"It always works out.
It rarely works out in the time frame or
manner we expect ... but it always works out."

Emily Matweow

Success is always on the other side of failure.
If you live your life without fear of losing it all,
you will be in the position to have everything to
gain.

Write Down:

The main things you are not willing to lose in life.

You will see that most things you have are for the
giving. The more you give away the more success
will reveal itself to you.

"When you are feeling down, broken, ravaged and lost, know you are living life bigger than yourself and you are not alone."

Jo Chubb

We always know the truth and yet we struggle and hold onto fear as the great comforter.

When you are at your lowest is when you know deep inside that you are closest to the truth and need to acknowledge you are not alone.

<u>Write down:</u>

- What are you controlling in your life due to fear?

- Now burn the paper and watch it evaporate into nothing.

Notes

"People forget how fast you did a job - but they remember how well you did it."

Howard Newton

EXERCISE

People connect emotionally to how they felt based on your action. People never forget how you made them feel.

Do everything you do with the intent to make people feel good.

Write Down

Who were the last 5 people you talked to?
Did you make them feel good?

"If you can educate your clients on one thing – what would it be?"

Fred Sarkari

<u>Write your answer here</u> (remember that the purpose of this is not simply to give information, but to educate).

N
o
t
e
s

"It is a bad plan that admits of no modification."

Publilius Syrus

Only when you see what works for you with fresh eyes, will you see how you can improve what is already working for you.

(Write Down)

— One thing you are doing or facing at this moment?

Use fresh eyes and look at it from all different perspectives.

> "Find the adventure in every day, revel in it, and be truly grateful for the experience."
>
> Lynda Norman

See the potential for a positive aspect to each and every experience, take it in fully, without judgement, savour the richness it is bringing to your life, and you will be filled with an amazing sense of gratitude.

A single moment has the power to change your life — be ready!

1. Make a conscious decision to find at least one adventure in your day.

2. Be grateful for the experience and share it enthusiastically with someone before the day is done.

3. Keep a list of all the amazing things that start coming into your life.

Notes

"Make the decision to smile and laugh more."

Fred Sarkari

People think of happiness as something they catch, like a cold. But it is more like a song, you have to practice it.

Print out large signs that say

Smile and Laugh

And place them everywhere you can. More importantly, practice it till it becomes a lifestyle.

(Write down:)

The people you come across who never smile or are pleasent.

Be their example by smiling at them with love whenever you see them.

"Expect the best from yourself, and nothing from others"

Arron Naylor

Stay focused on being the best you can be, and releasing others from your expectations and judgments.

Every time you judge someone, you are saying you are superior to them.

Answer the next two questions on the notes page.

1. What have you done today to be the best you can be?

2. Who have you judged today? Go apologize – even if they did not know you judged them.

"Invest in the best that resides within a person, then step back and watch them exceed every expectation."

Freyaz Shroff

Across countries, religions, gender, age, castes or financial prosperity, show people the good in them, illuminate their dreams, believe in them; they will create miracles with their lives and magic in the world!

1. Make a list of the people in your professional /personal life.
2. For each of them — identify what is the best within them.
3. How will you specifically invest in them?

"Like what you do, do what you like
and live life with Love!"

Charlie Aiken

E
X
E
R
C
I
S
E

By living the above quote, you will not only live an authentic life, you will protect the most valuable thing you have.

There is only one thing in this world that you cannot lose due to environment, economy or any situation out of your control and that is your word – it can only be lost if you alone are willing to sacrifice it for the lesser good.

Write Down

When was the last time you devalued your own word to yourself or another?

Drop everything and go take accountability for it right now!

'What is the purpose?"

Andrea Thatcher

E
X
E
R
C
I
S
E

With so many ways to answer any question you have, when you further ask the question 'what is the purpose' the true answer will appear.

<u>Write down</u>

Everything you are doing.

Ask yourself, "What is the purpose?"

"You be what you want your children to be"

Zarrir Bhandara

We preach to our children, yet what we don't realize is that they only hear the message we give through our actions not our preaching.

1.) Write down the decisions you need to make.

2.) Ask yourself how you would want your children to decide.

Notes

> "Even when storm clouds are swirling in our lives, it is the knowing that the sun shines just beyond the horizon that gets us through"
>
> Darcy Vervynck

The sun gives us energy, invigorates us, makes us feel alive and puts a smile on our face.

Make a list

1. Of all the 'Suns' in your life?
2. Create pictures of them
3. Place them everywhere and anywhere

During your darkest moments, you will be reminded that the sun exists right around the corner.

"Cherish every moment like it is a lifetime within itself"

Fred Sarkari

EXERCISE

I have always been amazed by how my nephew pours his heart into any task he faces. From practicing soccer to doing extra homework on his own time.

Respect yourself enough to pour your heart into the tasks that often seem inconsequential — the ones that no one else is aware of.

Those are the ones that define you from the inside out.

We are so busy anticipating what the next moment will bring or what we need to do to prepare for it that we miss the essence and beauty of the very moment we are presently in.

In turn, we lose out on life long connections and love for what we do and those around us.

Write Down

What moments do you know you should be cherishing more?

Notes

"We glorify birth and death, yet it's our soul's energetic trip between those stages which deserves the most tribute."

I have experienced 2 births and my father's passing. The two experiences were incredibly similar, not only with the intensity of emotion, but in the actual recognition of a person's energy, love, and spirit.

Our spirit has entered during birth, and experiences everything that life has to offer. This is the true celebration of life.

Dorota Katarzyna Ulkowska

Write Down

What and who are you celebrating in your life?

"Another adventure on the road of life."

Richard Montgomery

Life is not meant to be an accumulation of tasks completed everyday.

Life is meant to be a reminder to do something new. An accumulation of experiences based on new adventures.

Write Down

1. When was the last time you had an adventure?

2. If you could choose any adventure, what would it be?

Now plan to make it happen, as that is what life is all about.

Notes

> ## "Why lie to yourself,
> ## when you already know the truth."
>
> ### Scott Butt

At times it is easier to dress things up and make things more elaborate than they are.

Why do we waste time trying to lie, or fool ourselves into believing something that we know deep inside is not the truth?

<u>Be totally honest: Write Down</u>

1. What have you been lying to yourself about?

2. Why are you afraid of the truth?

3. What will happen if you face the truth and authentically live it?

EXERCISE

"One man's courage is another's leap of faith."

Ariella Tsafatinos

E
X
E
R
C
I
S
E

Courageous people are those who are willing to open themselves up and reveal their heart - their true selves.

They are willing to be imperfect and let go of who they think they should be in order to become who they are truly meant to be.

Be honest with yourself: Write Down

- In what specific part of your life have you not been who you know you should be ?

Be specific in what, deep inside, you know you are meant to be.

- 78 -

Notes

"HAVE FUN"

Mads Claussen

EXERCISE

I send my swimmers of to European Championships with "HAVE FUN" as the last words they hear from me.

Write Down:

1.) The things you are doing that are weighing you down.

2.) How can you start having fun with them?

Ask yourself, are you living this everyday?

"A man cannot be comfortable
without his own approval."

Mark Twain

Only when you learn to truly love yourself
can you love the important people in your
life - and it is only then that you can be
happy in your own skin.

Loving yourself means opening your heart without
judgment to every part of you - the good, the bad
and the ugly

Write Down:

- Where do you judge yourself?
- Find the good in all you have been judging
  and never stop until you do.

- 81 -

N
o
t
e
s

"Communication is not when the message gets sent, communication occurs only when the message is received."

Shayne Mauricette

In the information age, there's a lot of chatter both online and off but how much of that actually qualifies as communication as opposed to noise?

When communicating always remember:

(1.) Meanings are in people not in words. We interpret words emotionally based on our past experiences.

(2.) What you say either coincides or conflicts with how you say it. People will never forget how you made them feel — but they will forget what you said within seconds.

Write Down

(1.) People you have had a hard time communicating with

(2.) What can YOU do better?

"If there were only 3 messages you can share with your children what would they be?

Fred Sarkari

Write your answer here.

1.

2.

3.

"Have faith in what you love;
continue doing it with passion and it will
take you to where you wish to be!"

Carla Hampshire

Have faith and believe in yourself. Others may inspire you but only YOU can continue strong on that path you have chosen.

Write Down

1) All the things you love to do.

2) Who inspires you on that journey?

3) What drives you to continue your journey?

Never lose sight of that as it will be your anchor during stormy times.

"Have a vision of your life that is way beyond what you think you can do and be fearless."

Rosemary Smyth

There are 3 simple steps to fulfilling a life worth living.

1.) What is your vision? What are you trying to leave on this earth?

2.) Have the courage to share it with everyone that crosses your path.

3.) Live every moment of your life around your vision.

Your vision should encompass all aspects of your critical life.

Notes

"Surround yourself with positive people
who inspire you and uplift you to
your greatest potential"

Sarah Esch

They say that we are the average of the 5 people we spend the most time with. We are a product of our environment.

Write down:

1. 5 people you spend most of your time with
2. 2 things that are inspiring about each of them.
3. 2 things that are not what you would consider positive about them.

You have just looked at yourself in the mirror.

The hardest thing for humans to do is to let go.

Give yourself permission to "fire friends" and stop nursing relationships that do not serve you.

EXERCISE

"All people want results, very few fall in love
with what it takes to get the results."

Fred Sarkari

EXERCISE

I remember the worst course of treatment I
have undergone. It lasted 2 months fulltime
and I threw up almost every other day.

I so badly wanted the results but after a
few weeks I was fading and ready to quit.
That is when Michael (an incredible monk and
therapist) looked at me and said, "if you want
the results bad enough, you will have to start
falling in love with the process and journey."

Write Down On The Notes Pages,

What do you want so bad you can sense it in
every molecule of your body?

Now start falling in love with every aspect of
the journey it takes to get there.

"To succeed as a team is to hold all of the members accountable for their expertise."

Mitchell Caplan

If you want your people to be accountable give them something to be accountable for.

1. Make a list of your people.

2. Tell them specifically what you want them to be accountable for.

3. Get them to reiterate for clarification and ownership.

"In the business world, the rearview mirror is always clearer than the windshield."

Warren Buffett

Everything that you need to know about success can be learned from your history.

Make a list of: Everything that has worked for you in the past.

Now see how you can refine it and re-implement it.

"Management is nothing more than
motivating other people."

Lee Iacocca

Motivation is how you make your people feel on a
daily basis. Do not make it complicated — make
people feel like there is purpose within their role.

① Make a list of your people.

② Beside each, write their key motivator.

③ If you do not know, then you have just found
your main objective.

"First weigh the considerations,
then take the risks."

Helmuth von Moltke

Write down

Your strategy on top of the page and create 3 columns below.

1. In column one, write down all the possible outcomes.

2. In the second column, note if the outcome is positive or negative.

3. The third column is where you will identify how it will impact your business.

Notes

"If people aren't going to talk about your product, then it's not good enough."

Jeffrey Kalmikoff

Be bold. Your products and services need to have an impact and leave an impression.

1. Decide what you want people to say about your products and services.

2. Do your products/services reflect what you want people to say?

3. If not, what can you do to refine your product/service to reflect what you want people to say?

"There is nothing more attractive then a woman who wears her confidence with grace."

Fred Sarkari

I am never more proud than to see my niece embody this statement.

Most women have falsely come to believe that confidence is the same as arrogance and strength.

Natasha embodies true confidence with her grace, kindness and vibrancy. Her internal beauty lights up any room she enters.

Make A List

Of all the things you know you should be confident about.

Notes

"Many a small thing has been made large by the right kind of advertising."

Mark Twain

Having the best product, the best value, and the best price mean absolutely nothing if you do not <u>understand the psychology of marketing</u>.

1. All buying decisions are made on an emotional level.
2. 92% of those decisions are made at an unconscious level.
3. The only way to tap into the unconscious is repetition.

Now make sure you put all 3 of those together in your marketing.

— 101 —

"A business, like an automobile, has to be driven in order to get results."

B. C. Forbes

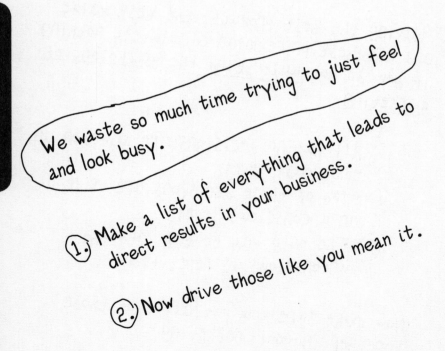

We waste so much time trying to just feel and look busy.

1. Make a list of everything that leads to direct results in your business.

2. Now drive those like you mean it.

"I rate enthusiasm even above professional skill."

Edward Appleton

EXERCISE

People will follow pure enthusiasm through even the most dire of situations.

1. Make a list of all the people around you.

2. What is the one thing you can be enthusiastic about with each of them?

Your enthusiasm will infect everyone with a desired purpose to follow your lead.

> "I'm not a driven businessman,
> but a driven artist. I never think about money.
> Beautiful things make money."
>
> Lord Acton

Treat your business like it is your art. As an artist in your business you will be able see things with a creative mind that most never will.

Write Down

If you were an artist, what kind of an artist would you be?

Now incorporate that into every aspect of your business.

Notes

"Live your life loud and don't let anyone
tell you to turn it down"!

Julie Clitheroe

The one consistency that I see in most people is that
they choose to live their lives for others over living it for
themselves.

They dress to please others, they buy cars to please
others, buy homes to please others...

Write down:

1. What do you honestly believe you are doing for
others more than for yourself?

2. What is it that you would like to do for yourself
that you are not because of what others might
think?

Go ahead and have the courage to do it for yourself.

"It's easy to make a buck. It's a lot tougher to make a difference."

Tom Brokaw

Make today the day you go home knowing you've made a difference in someone's life!

It only takes a few seconds to impact a life forever

For the next week —at the end of each day write down the specific difference you made in the lives of others.

Notes

> "Success or failure in business is caused more
> by the mental attitude even than
> by mental capacities."

> Walter Scott

EXERCISE

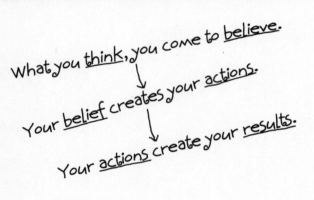

What you <u>think</u>, you come to <u>believe</u>.

Your <u>belief</u> creates your <u>actions</u>.

Your <u>actions</u> create your <u>results</u>.

Write Down

1. What kind of thoughts cross your mind everyday?

2. Results you want

Are your thoughts consistent to the results you want?

"There is only one boss: the customer.
And he can fire everybody in the company
from the chairman on down, simply by spending
his money somewhere else."

Sam Walton

People often think of customer service as a department, but the reality is that customer service is a <u>state of mind</u> that needs to **flow** through your entire business.

<u>Write down</u>

(1.) Every point of customer contact in your business.

Give your customers a reason at every point of contact to sing your praises.

Notes

"It's all about the relationship between gold and gunpowder."

Nick Kossavan

The constant struggle with my inner demons resulted in me stammering these words during a boozed fueled philosophical conversation.

It's the constant hunt to find a co-existing relationship between our inner wants and outer demands that creates the forward momentum for our journey.

1. Make a list of all your inner wants that you have hidden deep within you due to all the demands in your life.

2. Pick one of them and start working towards it.

EXERCISE

"Never ask anyone to do something you yourself are not willing to do."

Sandra Bastain

EXERCISE

The greatest leaders I ever worked with had one thing in common. They were all _willing_ to do what they asked of me to do.

Write Down

What are you expecting your people to do that you have not proven you are _willing_ to do if need be?

At times, let them see you do what you are asking them to do.

Notes

"Whenever an individual or a business decides that success has been attained, progress stops."

Thomas J. Watson

Make a list

(1.) What is working in your business.

(2.) Now make a list of what is not working in your business.

How can you refine both lists?

If what is not working cannot be refined — drop it and drive the stuff that is.

"Wise are those who learn that the bottom line doesn't always have to be their top priority."

William Arthur Ward

You will be so much happier if you let money be the by-product of building a business with integrity.

(1.) What does the reputation of your business mean to you? <u>Write down whatever comes to mind.</u>

(2.) Now take whatever steps necessary to protect it against all odds.

Notes

> "If you really want something, make it happen.
> If you won't make it happen, you might not
> want it as much as you think you do."

Krista Barzso

Stop wasting all your years thinking about what you want to do. Either start working towards it or let it go and move forward.

In high school, Frank wanted to be a veterinarian. I ran into Frank in my last year of University, he still wanted to be a veterinarian. 7 years later I ran into Frank, he still talked about wanting to be a veterinarian.

I wonder if he ever did?

Make a list of:

All the things you always wanted to do or make happen.

Pick one that resonates most with you now. Believe you can make it into a reality. What is the first step you need to take. Now just take it.

"Die trying - as not trying is death in itself."

Fred Sarkari

Next time you feel like you are tired, that you've hit the end of the road and are ready to give up, believe you are better than that. We always have something more within us to keep moving forward.

Write Down

① What drives you. - your reason WHY.

Write it down everywhere and never. ever lose sight of it.

It is your oxygen. without it you/your business will die.

Notes

"Do more than is required. What is the distance between someone who achieves their goals consistently and those who spend their lives and careers merely following? The extra mile."

Gary Ryan Blair

For the next week ask yourself

①. What more can I do for the person in front of me?

②. How can I make this moment memorable for them?'

That is going the extra mile.

"I want to put a ding in the universe."

Steve Jobs

Write Down

The first thing that comes to mind when you read the words.

"What is my legacy?"

Now re-write it without trying to sound fancy.

"Leave behind a legacy of compassion."

Fred Sarkari

This is my legacy -want to know yours?
Write your own eulogy and work backwards.

"If one does not know to which port one is sailing, no wind is favorable."

Lucius Annaeus Seneca

It makes no sense to spend hours and days and weeks and years trying to get somewhere if you have no clear idea where you are trying to get to in the first place.

Keep it simple and just <u>write down</u> where you want to end up – Write whatever comes to mind for all aspects of your life.

Now ask yourself, what are you specifically doing to get there?

Notes

"Do not live for what you did in the past, live for what you know deep inside is the kind of person you are capable of being."

Fred Sarkari

If you knew you could not fail, what would you do differently? How would you run your business? How would you love?

Write anything that comes to mind.

> "A creative man is motivated by the desire to achieve, not by the desire to beat others."
>
> Ayn Rand

The most enjoyable and memorable triathlon I ever participated in was the half-Ironman I did while injured.

(I ran my own race.)

I did not try to compete with anyone else. I laughed and smiled and enjoyed every minute while staying focused on the moment.

<u>Write down:</u>

1.) All the parts in your life where you are more focused on beating others?

2.) If you can't think of any — think again as we all get caught up with this in our lives.

3.) Pick one of them and always stay aware of achieving for the sake of achieving and not beating others.

Notes

"One person with a belief is equal to a force of ninety-nine who have only interests."

Peter Marshall

The best people who have ever worked for me are the ones who believed in my vision.

The only way your people can believe in your vision is if you have one to share.

Write out your vision, which is nothing more than your mantra of why you do what you do.

Your vision is useless if you don't have the courage to share it with everyone.

"Millions saw the apple fall, but Newton
was the one who asked why."

Bernard Baruch

You will **find** that most of the things
you do make you feel perpetually busy
with no results.

1.) Break down every step in your
business.

2.) Look at each and ask yourself
why you are doing it.

Notes

"The world is full of people who were laughed at only to eventually move humanity forward."

Ivan Sampson

EXERCISE

Next time someone laughs at your ideas, smile – you know you are doing the right thing, and any dead fish can float downstream.

Write down:

All the ideas that still sit within you but you've never put forward because of what other's would think.

- Pick one you can start with and enjoy the laughter. Let it remind you that you are doing somehting different and living your life.

"Obstacles are things a person sees when he takes his eyes off his goal."

E. Joseph Cossman

Obstacles are only 2 things:

1.) An excuse to give up

2.) A reason to be creative

Outcome, in any situation, is very predictable as it is based on these 2 possibilities only.

Write down:

A list of all the obstacles you are facing in life (keep writing)

Which ones have you truly given up on? (Be honest)

Pick the one you would like to work through and ask yourself "how can I be more creative with this?"

Notes

"Look up to the sky and know
you can write your name in it."

Fred Sarkari

What do you want to be remembered for?

Be as specific as possible — write whatever
comes to mind.

E
X
E
R
C
I
S
E

"Action is the foundational key to all success."

Pablo Picasso

My attitude kept me alive for years when no one believed in me. Then I noticed a decade later I was still in the same spot I started at.

The right attitude without action is nothing more than a hamster-wheel fantasy.

1. Identify one thing that has been a _perpetual_ obstacle or challenge in your life.

2. Write down specifically what action you need to take to fix it.

3. Start now, one inch at a time.

"Defeat is not the worst of failures.
Not to have tried is the true failure."

George Edward Woodberry

1.) Write down all the times you believe you have been defeated.

2.) Now write down all the good that came out of those situations.

If you can't think of any good outcome then change your mindset and try again.

"Don't confuse fame with success.
Madonna is one; Helen Keller is the other."

Erma Bombeck

1.) Create 2 columns - Success and Fame.

2.) Write down all the parts of you that fall under each heading.

A great way to look in the mirror!

"Don't aim for success if you want it;
just do what you love and believe in,
and it will come naturally."

David Frost

It breaks my heart every time I meet
someone who says 'I would love to do...' –

I would rather chase what I love, and risk
never receiving, than live with the regret
that I was too spineless to even try.

What would you love to do that you are
not doing?

"Do not let your past control your present
and future, use it to grow and
control your own destiny."

Fred Sarkari

1.) <u>Write down</u> the moments that you think have defined you throughout your life.

2.) Now re-create your identity, your story, your destiny through those moments.

"All our dreams can come true,
if we have the courage to pursue them."

Walt Disney

E X E R C I S E

You have a dream that has been inside of you for an eternity. Spend every day pursuing it. Just do not place it in a box deep inside your heart.

Write down all the dreams you've wanted to achieve ever since you were a child.

"Any idiot can face a crisis - its day to day living that wears you out."

Anton Chekhov

Just stop and take a breath before you react from one crazy moment to another. They will never end so you might as well learn to enjoy them with ease. We are so focused on getting to the next moment that we lose sight of the beauty right in front of us.

Start every day with 5 things you know have to be done in order to have LIVED your day.

Hugging a loved one should be one of them.

Write the 5 things down on the notes page

"Every man dies. Not every man really lives."

William Wallace

As a child, your world existed in a room full of toys. Treat your world as such. Laugh and play with everything around you.

Being too serious and grown up ultimately destroys all the joy around you.

Write Down

What are you too serious about?

> "All lasting business is built on friendship."

> Alfred A. Montapert

E
X
E
R
C
I
S
E

Have the courage to open your heart and truly care for the people in your business. Know that most might disappoint you but it is all worth it for those few who will create everlasting joy in both your business and your life.

1.) Make a list of the people in your business.

2.) What part of their friendship do you value?

3.) Now go and share it with them.

> "The art of living is more like wrestling than dancing."
>
> Marcus Aurelius

If you can learn any kind of dancing, what would it be? Now dance, or go learn to dance. Dancing is vitamins for the soul.

I would love to be able to dance
_____

"A man who wants to lead the orchestra must turn his back on the crowd."

Max Lucado

If you want to live a fulfilling life, you have to be willing to turn your back on what is considered normal.

Design your own life for your own needs — and live your own true authentic life everyday.

Write Down

A story that describes a part of the authentic life you want.

For you artistic people, draw out a collage of that life.

"You may only have one life but the way you spend it is up to you."

Natasha Chinoy
(My 13 year old niece)

I, as a child, have a lot of dreams. I hope never to forget them as most adults do.

①. <u>Write down</u> all the things you want to do in life.

②. Keep writing and never stop adding to the list.

③. Spend every season crossing 1 off the list.

"If you don't control your anger
it will control you"

Zal Chinoy
(My 11 year old nephew)

Why do grown ups get angry so easily? Don't they
know we are watching and learning?

1. <u>Write down</u> the 3 things you get angry about
all the time.

2. Ask yourself why you really do?

3. Everytime you face the same situation, know
children are watching.

"Just be a little happier."

Fred Sarkari

If you need an explanation on this you have even bigger issues to consider - Just be a little happier means simply that - just be a little happier.

KEYNOTES AND SEMINARS WITH FRED

Considered an expert in human behavior, Fred Sarkari coaches, teaches and provides management consulting services from start-ups to some of the world's largest organizations.

He is the president of a unique sales and personal development company that *Inspires* and *Educates* individuals / organizations to *Execute* their ideas.

Fred remains highly active in providing individuals with ongoing one-on-one coaching, from goal setting to execution.

Fred has facilitated numerous workshops for employees of - Microsoft, Wells Fargo, BMW, Scotia Bank, Coca-Cola, Home Depot, CIBC, Royal Bank, North West Mutual Funds, Ceridian, Promotional Products Association, BMO Bank of Montreal, Genworth Financial, Hilton Hotels, Midas, Four Seasons Hotels and many more.

www.FredSarkari.com

800.742.2379

Fred@fredsarkari.com

OTHER BOOKS AND WEBSITES

"How The Top 5% Think" – Principles of Great Leaders.

"Courage To Be Naked" – The Ultimate Guide To Presenting and Communicating Your Message.

Join our Newsletter on
www.FredSarkari.com

BLOG: www.MentalSidewalk.com

Join us on Facebook.com/FredSarkari

www.ZanaBooks.com